BEHOLD, YOUR MOTHER!

a teen girl's reflections on the Holy Rosary

Grace E. Belle-Oudry

FRANCIS
Publishing Co.

**Behold, Your Mother!
a teen girl's reflections on the Holy
Rosary**

Grace E. Belle-Oudry

COVER IMAGE: L'Innocence by William-Adolphe Bouguereau

ISBN 978-0615793382

First Edition

10 9 8 7 6 5 4 3 2 1

For reorders;
beholdyourmotherbook@gmail.com

Published by FRANCIS Publishing Company
Arizona, USA

Dedicated to John Szilagy, for
all of the Rosaries we prayed
together.
Thanks for being my adopted
Grandpa. I will always remember
you and that smile of yours! May you
rest in peace.
Love,
"Amazing Grace"

I have known Grace Belle-Oudry since she was a little girl. I have always seen something special in her. I remember noticing a rare sweetness about her the very first time I met her. That sweetness, thank God, remains to this day.

I was delighted to learn, as Grace grew older, that she has a love for writing like I do. She writes all kinds of wonderful things, including some great fiction, which I have no doubt, the world will be reading someday.

But here, in this book, she presents the world with a nonfiction treasure. Through this rosary prayer book, Grace shares with you a bit of her heart. Actually, a great deal of her heart. I know she hopes for one thing above all – that the prayers she has penned brings you closer to God. I join my prayers with Grace's for this intention. May you find this book a blessing for your journey, a light to your path leading to Jesus, accompanied by the love of our Blessed Mother.

~Sherry Boas
Author of *The Lily Trilogy, Wing Tip*, and *A Mother's Bouquet: Rosary Meditations for Moms.*

INTRODUCTION:

Archbishop Fulton J. Sheen once said, *"The power of the Rosary is beyond description."* St. Padre Pio called the Rosary *"The greatest weapon we have."* The Blessed Virgin Mary told St. Dominic *"Through the Rosary [and the Scapular] I will save the world."*

The Rosary is a set of prayers recited on beads. It was originally given by Our Lady to St. Dominic in 1208 A.D. The Rosary is like a beautiful bouquet of prayers offered to Our Lady that spiritually links us to her Son Jesus, and it is also a beautiful way to meditate on the Bible. Think about it: the Angel Gabriel was the first one to say *"Hail, full of grace, the Lord is with you!" (Luke 1:28)* and St. Elizabeth, who was both Mary's cousin and St. John the Baptist's mother, exclaimed *"Blessed are you among women and blessed is the Fruit of your womb!" (Luke 1:42).* Jesus taught the Apostles how to pray the Our Father (or Lord's Prayer) in *Matthew 6:9-15.* Our Lady of Fatima told the children to pray the "O my Jesus" (or Fatima prayer) when they recited their daily Rosaries. She also told them to pray the Rosary *every day* for world peace, and specifically for the conversion of Russia.

Even in ancient times, before the Blessed Virgin appeared to St. Dominic, monks in Ireland prayed a sort of Rosary by counting pebbles as they prayed one hundred-fifty psalms. However, the laypeople complained that they couldn't remember the psalms since they couldn't read. The monks told them to pray one hundred-fifty Our Fathers. They also began reciting "Psalters of Our Lord and Savior Jesus Christ," which were meditative praises on the life of Our Lord. Then they made a set for the Blessed Virgin. They soon shortened it to fifty, which was called *"Rosarium,"* meaning "bouquet."

Although you are probably very busy with family and texting, friends and texting, school and texting, chores and texting, the Rosary really only takes about fifteen minutes to pray. That's like half the time it takes to watch a TV show, and it'll help you get to Heaven, too! Praying the Rosary with your family will bring you all closer. I'm sure that soon you will find yourself falling in love with the Rosary and trying to "sneak" one in here and there.

Try praying the Rosary with your friends. You may be surprised just how willing they are to pray with you. All you have to do is ask.

Of course it's always nice to pray the Rosary in front of the Blessed Sacrament in the adoration chapel, but sometimes that's easier said than done. Life is full of duties and responsibilities and God knows that. So, after you do what you have to, try to step into the chapel to pray your Rosary. If you really can't make it to the chapel, you can always go to www.Savior.org. As of this writing in 2013, they have live streaming Eucharistic adoration 24/7— you can pray in front of your computer screen, and it will almost be like you're there, reciting your Rosary in the chapel!

I've been praying the Rosary ever since I *can't* remember... my mom used to pray the Scriptural Rosary (a Bible verse before each Hail Mary) every day before I was born, and she's always encouraged me to recite the Rosary. When I was thirteen in early 2011, she and I started visiting nursing homes, hospitals, and hospices to pray the Rosary with the residents/patients who lived there. The first time we were about to give it a try, she asked if I would go with her and our pal Phyllis to the nursing home to pray with a Catholic man named John. I was beyond scared and really did not want to go. I did anyway, but just to be done with it and so I wouldn't have that "hanging over" my head for years to come. Well, that one little decision changed my life in so many positive ways and it made me a much better person! John and I ended up becoming VERY good friends; both of my grandfathers died young, before I was born, so I thought of John as my grandfather, and he called me "Amazing Grace"☺. Mom, Phyllis, and I started visiting John once a week. As he got sicker, and as he and I got closer, we started visiting him every day!

John had been an English teacher and a farmer, and he was also a very funny man (he used to say to me, "You're beautiful! I bet all the little boys at church chase after you, don't they?" and when I said, "No, they don't," he'd reply "They're crazy!" and wink), and he was also talented. He once received money at the nursing home after winning their talent contest by singing "*Old Man River*," and we often sang church hymns together. John and I had a lot in common.

He was amazed when one day while we were visiting, a commercial for the movie *Ben-Hur* came on the television. He said, "Do you know who that actor is?" and I responded, "Yes; Charlton Heston." After the initial shock of a fourteen year-old knowing who Charlton Heston was, he told me that he went to the same high school as him and often saw him walking through the halls!

Now western movies are not my favorite, (I'm a native Arizonan; I don't have to be reminded that there's dirt everywhere), but one day I watched a movie called *Rio Bravo* because my absolute most favorite singers (Dean Martin and Ricky Nelson) starred in it. Some weeks later John said something about how he loved watching westerns, so I took the opportunity to ask if, by any chance, he had seen *Rio Bravo.* He told me that it was his favorite movie! And he said that he would love to watch it with me. I looked for it on DVD on *Amazon.com* and got quite a shock. It cost $85! That night, going to bed, I thought how I wished that I could buy *Rio Bravo* so I could watch it with John. (At this point, he was becoming sicker and sicker every day). I prayed about it before falling asleep. The next day we were at *Wal-Mart*, and you'd never guess what I found in one of those beloved five-dollar movie bins (that usually just have *Barbie* movies)... *Rio Bravo!!!* Needless to say, I bought it.

Unfortunately, John passed away before we got a chance to watch it together. But whenever I watch *Rio Bravo* (which is too often, I'm afraid) I always feel like John's up there, watching it with me as I stare in wide-eyed amazement while Dean and Ricky sing "*My Rifle, My Pony, and Me.*"

HOW TO USE THIS BOOK:

There are dozens of ways to use this book! You can simply pray the Rosary and read the reflections of the mysteries at each decade, you can read one every morning when you wake up and focus on those thoughts throughout the day, or you can pray the Rosary with a group and have each person read a reflection aloud. The possibilities are endless, so get creative!

If you'd like to break-up the reflections and just recite the prayers I've written or just the scripture verse pertaining to the decade, I've made a handy little legend for you to use to easily access what you need.

The ☀ (sun) as Jesus is the "Light of the world" indicates the scripture verse.

The ♥ (heart) indicates the prayer.

The ▉ (thought bubble) indicates the reflection.

Another possibility is to repeat the Scripture verse and/or mystery before each Hail Mary.

Or using the religious pictures of each Mystery for meditation is another way to use this book to pray the Rosary.

Sunday and Wednesday--Glorious Mysteries

Monday and Saturday--Joyful Mysteries

Tuesday and Friday--Sorrowful Mysteries

Thursday--Luminous Mysteries

PRAYERS OF THE ROSARY:

Sign of the Cross: In the Name of the Father, and of the Son, and of the Holy Spirit. Amen.

Apostles' Creed: I believe in God, the Father almighty, Creator of Heaven and earth, and in Jesus Christ, His only Son, Our Lord, Who was conceived by the Holy Spirit, born of the Virgin Mary, suffered under Pontius Pilate, was crucified, died, and was buried; He descended into hell; on the third day He rose again from the dead; He ascended into Heaven, and is seated at the right hand of God the Father almighty; from there He will come to judge the living and the dead. I believe in the Holy Spirit, the holy catholic Church, the communion of saints, the forgiveness of sins, the resurrection of the body, and life everlasting. Amen.

Glory Be: Glory be to the Father and to the Son, and to the Holy Spirit, as it was in the beginning is now and ever shall be, world without end. Amen.

Our Father: Our Father, Who art in Heaven, hallowed be Thy Name. Thy kingdom come, Thy will be done, on earth as it is in Heaven. Give us this day our daily bread and forgive us our trespasses, as we forgive those who trespass against us, and lead us not into temptation, but deliver us from evil. Amen.

Hail Mary: Hail Mary, full of grace, the Lord is with thee. Blessed art thou among women and blessed is the Fruit of thy womb, Jesus. Holy Mary, Mother of God, pray for us sinners now and at the hour of our death. Amen.

Fatima Prayer: O my Jesus, forgive us our sins, save us from the fires of hell, lead all souls to Heaven, especially those in most need of Thy mercy. Amen.

Hail, Holy Queen: Hail Holy Queen, Mother of Mercy, our life, our sweetness, and our hope! To thee do we cry, poor banished children of Eve, to thee do we send up our sighs, mourning and weeping in this valley of tears. Turn then, most gracious advocate, thine eyes of mercy towards us, and after this our exile, show unto us the blessed Fruit of thy womb, Jesus. O clement, O loving, O sweet Virgin Mary! Pray for us, O Holy Mother of God. That we may be made worthy of the promises of Christ.

Concluding Prayer: O God, Whose only begotten Son, by His life, death, and resurrection, has purchased for us the rewards of eternal salvation, grant, we beseech Thee, that while meditating upon these mysteries in the most holy Rosary of the Blessed Virgin Mary, we may imitate what they contain and obtain what they promise, through the same Christ Our Lord. Amen.

HOW TO PRAY THE ROSARY:

While holding the Crucifix, make the Sign of the Cross. Then recite the Apostles' Creed.

Recite one Our Father on the first large bead. On each of the three small beads, recite a Hail Mary. Recite the Glory Be on the next large bead, followed by the Fatima prayer. Read the first Rosary mystery and meditation, and recite the Our Father on the next large bead.

On each of the next ten small beads (called a *decade*), recite the Hail Mary while reflecting on the current mystery. Continue until you have circled the entire Rosary (five decades). Or for a full Rosary, you will circle it four times (twenty decades).

Recite the Hail, Holy Queen and concluding prayers and make the Sign of the Cross.

The Joyful Mysteries

(to be recited on Mondays and Saturdays)

In the Joyful Mysteries we meditate on the **Annunciation** of the Angel Gabriel to Mary telling her that she would be the Mother of God.

We also reflect on the **Visitation** of Mary to her cousin Elizabeth, who, even at an old age, was expecting to give birth to St. John the Baptist.

We meditate on Jesus' Birth, the **Nativity,** in a humble little stable in Bethlehem.

We contemplate the **Presentation** of Jesus in the Temple as an infant and the **Finding of Jesus in the Temple** when He was 12 years old.

FIRST JOYFUL MYSTERY
THE ANNUNCIATION

"May it be done unto me"
~Luke 1:38

My Beautiful Savior, grant, I ask You, the virtues of obedience and humility. Give me the obedience to do Your will in everything that I do, whether it be getting dressed, playing sports, or going on the computer. Give to me that perfect obedience Your Blessed Mother Mary had when she said "yes" to God the Father. I long for that obedience.

A young teenager named Mary was asked by God the Father through the Angel Gabriel to be the Mother of God the Son. If He were to ask the same of me, would I respond with a "yes" as she did?

Let's ask Jesus to grant us all the humility to walk humbly side by side with Him in every instance of our lives, so that when this earthly life is over for us we may be one with Him forever in Heaven.

By meditating on the Annunciation may we all build a perfect dwelling place for Him in our souls, just as Mary did in her blessed womb. May this dwelling place be filled with good things and not worldliness or impurity. As St. Paul said:

"Whatever is good, whatever is true, whatever is honorable, whatever is just, whatever is pure, whatever is lovely, whatever is gracious, if there is any excellence, if there is anything worthy of praise, think about these things." (Philippians 4:8)

SECOND JOYFUL MYSTERY
THE VISITATION

"At the moment the sound of your greeting reached my ears, the infant in my womb leapt for joy."
~Luke 1:44

Jesus, meditating on the Visitation, I ask You for the gift of Joy. Not worldly joy in material things that will pass away, but Your perfect Joy. Let me find Your Joy in all things good, and help me give that Joy to everyone I meet.

Maybe some of your friends just don't get it. Ask the Holy Spirit to fill you, as He filled St. John the Baptist in his mother's womb, so that you may be Joyful when you talk to them. Ask God to allow this awesome Joy to fill them, so that they too might know, love, and serve Him.

Jesus, give us the Joy You gave Your Mother when she said, *"My soul proclaims the greatness of the Lord and my spirit exults in God my Savior, because He has looked upon His lowly handmaid." (Luke 1:46-48)*

Sometimes it's hard to be joyful. ESPECIALLY as a teenager.

There are so many things out there to want and *Amazon.com* is so tempting! A lot of times we may feel left out because of the way we dress or when we like things no one else seems to. Jesus, help us turn this craving for material things and social acceptance into longing for You Alone, for You are the only One Who can truly satisfy all our desires.

THIRD JOYFUL MYSTERY
THE BIRTH OF JESUS

"You will find an infant wrapped in swaddling clothes and lying in a manger."
~Luke 2:12

Jesus, let all my earthly desires be put aside so that I may link closer to You through Your lowly Nativity. Rather than longing for an *iPod* (which I do) or a trip to *Old Navy* (which I do), let me grow in humility and help others who are less privileged than I.

How sweet it must have been after Mary gave birth to Jesus to gaze into His Eyes! If you have ever held a newborn baby you know how amazing it is to see their little face and to feel their soft skin against yours. You know how it feels when they breathe and how every little movement they make seems so amazing. That being said, how could anyone say there isn't a God?!

Think about the perfect Humility of God. His only Son was born in a stable and had no place to lie except in a manger used to feed animals. The Supreme Being was born into poverty to show us how to practice Humility.

We can find Jesus in everyone we meet, especially the poor. Mother Teresa used to pick up dying people off the streets and care for them and love them, even if they lived for only a minute longer.

Would *I* do the same?

FOURTH JOYFUL MYSTERY
THE PRESENTATION OF JESUS

*"They took Him up to Jerusalem
to present Him to the Lord."
~Luke 2:22*

My Beautiful Savior, help me to be adorned
in purity as a palace is bedecked with jewels.
Help me to prepare a perfect dwelling place
for You, my Lord and Savior.

Our bodies are not our own, so we must take great care of them. We must dress modestly, since we are temples of the Holy Spirit and have Jesus dwelling within us. Kings do not live in dirty shacks but rather grand palaces; we need to strive to make our soul the greatest, purity-adorned palace we can.

When I am presented to the Lord, what will He find that I did wrong? Probably many things, since I am just a human being. But will He say that the palace I made for Him was impure and dirty?

To present the Lord into our temples we **must dress modestly**. We also must pay special attention to the care of the eternal palace, our souls. All our spiritual life dwells from our souls, so we must take great care of them.

"And when the parents brought in the child Jesus, he [Simeon] took Him into his arms and blessed God. 'Now, Master, You can let Your servant go in peace, just as You promised. Because my eyes have seen the salvation which You have prepared for all the nations to see.'" *(Luke 2:27-31)* When my nephew, Austin, was born, I felt like Simeon the first time I held him. I was at a loss for words and yet inside my soul was overflowing with love for and praises to God. If only everyone felt that way when they see a baby! It's only natural that we should praise God when we see what He created with His Love.

Let's pray this decade for all of the people who believe abortion is "health care". Pray that they may be converted to the truth. The fifth Commandment says, "Thou shall not Kill".

Let's also pray for people who think that physical appearance is everything. Let's pray for teens who think that to be cool or to fit-in with the rest of the crowd they have to dress immodestly.

FIFTH JOYFUL MYSTERY
FINDING JESUS IN THE TEMPLE

"When His parents saw Him, they were astonished, and His Mother said to Him, 'Son, why have You done this to us? Your father and I have been looking for You with great anxiety.' And He said to them, 'Why were you looking for Me? Did you not know that I must be in My Father's house?'"
~Luke 2:48-49

My Beautiful Savior, help me to find You in my life every day. I meet many people each day; help me to be kind to them and know that You dwell within them. Help me to be like St. Dominic Savio, a young boy who said, "I would rather die than commit a mortal sin." I want to lose everything in this passing world and I wish to gain Heaven, Your Father's House.

Joseph and Mary found Jesus *teaching* the *teachers* in the

Temple. We need to find Jesus in every person we meet. It's easy to see Him in innocent little babies or in your best friend. It's harder to find Him in some people. But He's in there! We need to treat each and every person we meet as if they were Jesus, because every one of us was created in the image and likeness of God. That means we have an eternal soul that will never die. St. Paul tells us that our bodies are *"Dwelling places of the Holy Spirit."* (1 Corinthians 6:19) It doesn't matter what color, shape or size a person is. God dwells in them whether they like it or not!

Today try to see Jesus in everyone you meet and treat them with the same loving respect you would give to Him.

The Luminous Mysteries

(to be recited on Thursdays)

In the Luminous Mysteries we meditate on the **Baptism of Jesus** by St. John the Baptist in the river Jordan.

We think about Jesus' first miracle in the **Wedding at Cana** where He changed water into wine.

We also meditate on the Proclamation of the **Kingdom of God** where Jesus tells us to *"Repent and believe in the Gospel"* (Mark 1:15).

We meditate on the **Transfiguration** where Moses and Elijah appeared with Jesus, Who is shown in all His glory before Peter, James, and John.

And last but certainly not least we meditate on the **Institution of the Eucharist** at the Last Supper, which was the first Mass.

FIRST LUMINOUS MYSTERY
THE BAPTISM OF OUR LORD

"Then Jesus came from Galilee to the Jordan to John, to be baptized by him. John would have prevented Him, saying 'I need to be baptized by You, and do You come to me?' But Jesus answered him 'Let it be so now; For thus it is fitting for us to fulfill all righteousness.' Then he consented."
~Matthew 3:13-15

My Wonderful Lord, help me to live by Your example and help me to be a good example to everyone I meet. Like Saint John, I know that You didn't need to be baptized; You never committed, or were ever capable of committing, a sin. Help me, a sinner, to always do what You would in every circumstance, so that I may win more souls for Your glory.

As Catholics we know how important the Sacrament of Baptism is for our souls. To be born physically we need to be in our mother's womb, but to be born spiritually we need to be baptized. Jesus Himself showed us how important this Sacrament is in the River Jordan with His cousin, Saint John the Baptist.

Infant baptism removes the original sin we are all born with ever since Adam and Eve disobeyed God's command to not eat of that one tree. An adult receiving this sacrament would have original sin removed and all of the sins they have ever committed. Obviously, Jesus never committed sin and was not born with original sin and did not need to be baptized.

So Jesus showed us how to live by His own example. He showed us how important baptism is by being baptized Himself. Let's follow His example and be a light for others.

SECOND LUMINOUS MYSTERY
THE WEDDING AT CANA

"When the wine ran short, the Mother of Jesus said to Him, 'They have no wine.' And Jesus said to her, 'Woman, how does your concern affect Me? My hour has not yet come.' His mother said to the servers, 'Do whatever He tells you.'"
~John 2:3-5

My Wonderful Lord, help me to always do what You tell me. Help me to silence this material world and bring my focus always to You.

Jesus' first miracle was at a wedding. This tells us so much about how wonderful the Sacrament of Matrimony is to God.

As tweens and teens, the world seems to scream at us "Go on a date!" The world's view on marriage is *very* different from God's.

When the world says "Start dating!" we should wait and *"Do whatever he tells [us]".*

Maybe marriage isn't your calling. Maybe your calling is to the religious life, or maybe you are called to the single life. Rather than thinking about dating, pray and ask God what it is He wants you to do. If marriage is in your future, take time to pray for your future spouse. Dating or courting should be reserved until we are older and ready for the spouse God intends for us to marry.

There is a movie from 1961 called *West Side Story,* and in one of the scenes the two main characters (Tony and Maria) see each other at a dance. Suddenly, everything around them fogs up until only they are left in the room (or so they think) staring at each other lovingly. This is how we should be with God and the world. Let the Holy Spirit cover the world with a fog, so that nothing else but God matters in your life.

THIRD LUMINOUS MYSTERY
THE PROCLAMATION
OF THE KINGDOM

"After John had been arrested, Jesus came to Galilee proclaiming the Gospel of God: 'This is the time of fulfillment. The kingdom of God is at hand. Repent, and believe in the Gospel.'"
~Mark 1:14-15

My Wonderful Lord, help me to *live* the Gospel in my life. Let it be for me a "user's manual" in this crazy, impure world. Let every move I make be for You and You alone.

What does Jesus mean by *"Believe in the Gospel"?* He is telling us that just reading the Bible is not enough. As Catholics, we need to firmly believe in everything the Bible says as is taught by the Magisterium of the Catholic Church.

St Augustine said, "If you believe what you like in the Gospels, and reject what you don't like, it is not the Gospel you believe, but yourself".

The basis of our Catholic Religion is the Bible. It really is a user's manual for us all. Sometimes the Bible seems challenging and like it was just written for old people, but it really isn't. If you take a few minutes every day to read the Bible (the New Testament is the best place to start) you will fall in love with it! It will make clearer sense to you and you will realize what an awesome God we have. Through the Gospels He set us up with everything we need.

The pastor at my parish (the wonderful Fr. Thomas Bennett) once told us that he received his first Bible when he was eleven. His mother wrote inside it, "this book will keep you from sin, and sin will keep you from this book."

Take this time to meditate on this and really make the Gospel your spiritual "food."

FOURTH LUMINOUS MYSTERY
THE TRANSFIGURATION

*"Lord, it is good that we
are here."*
~Matthew 17:4

My Wonderful Lord, how often
do I try to make myself comfortable in
this world! But I know that true comfort
is life in Heaven with You for all eternity. I
understand what Peter, James, and John
must have felt when they wanted to stay
with You on top of the mountain. My
Jesus, flow Your heavenly love into me so
that I may bring You to others and not
just "bottle You up" for myself alone.

Ever think "this world
stinks!"? Okay, it's partly true. But
that's not because God made it that
way. We humans made this world
impure and materialistic. *We made* it
a place of sadness and poverty when
Eve disobeyed God's one and only
command. We needed a Savior to
come and save us from our sins. And

our all-merciful, all-knowing, all-loving God knew that. We could never make it on our own; if God stopped thinking of you for one single half of a moment you wouldn't be alive. So, really, it *is* good that we are here!

We teens have a HUGE impact on culture through music, movies, fashion, language, etc. We need to make sure that impact is *positive*— if we use these earthly things carefully and wisely and for the good of the Church, we can change the world for the better. Just by reciting this Rosary right now, you are bringing good into the world; returning God's love for all o f the evil out there. Even though it might be hard to say "Lord, it is good that we are here" when we live in a world with poverty and crime, with hunger and pain, we can change those things through *prayer.*

FIFTH LUMINOUS MYSTERY
INSTITUTION OF THE
HOLY EUCHARIST

"Jesus took the bread, said the blessing, broke it, and giving it to His disciples said: 'Take and eat. This is My Body.' Then He took a cup, gave thanks, and gave it to them, saying: 'Drink from it, all of you, for this is the Blood of the Covenant, which will be shed on behalf of many for the forgiveness of sins.'"
~Matthew 26:26-27

My Wonderful Lord, I thank You for the beautiful gift of the Holy Eucharist. I know that without it I could not function. I want to make the Eucharist my Everything. And You know that, Lord, Who are all-knowing and all-powerful.

So I'm pretty sure the coolest word I've ever heard, spelled, or read is *transubstantiation*. And what a miracle it is!

Under the "form" of ordinary bread and wine, Jesus becomes truly present; BODY, BLOOD, SOUL, AND DIVINITY. What does this mean for us? It means sharing in the life of Jesus. He loves us so much He offers Himself to us through the Holy Eucharist. What perfect charity, perfect love, perfect mercy! Even if you can't receive daily Communion, you can receive Him spiritually through an Act of Spiritual Communion.

St. Maximilian Kolbe said, "God dwells in our midst, in the Blessed Sacrament of the altar". Make sacrifices every day for your family, friends *and enemies.* Jesus did so when He instituted the Eucharist at the Last Supper, the first Mass.

The Sorrowful Mysteries

In the Sorrowful Mysteries we meditate on the passion and death of Jesus Christ.

First, we meditate on the **Agony of Our Lord in the Garden** of Gethsemane, where He prayed so fervently *"His sweat became like drops of blood"* as He awaited His Crucifixion.

Then we go to **the Scourging** of Our Lord at the Pillar, where He was stripped of His clothing, beaten, and spat upon by the Roman soldiers.

Then we meditate on the **Crowning of** Our Lord's precious Head with **thorns,** causing Him excruciating pain.

Fourthly, we meditate on the **Carrying of the Cross,** where Our

Lord carried the heavy wood cross to the place called Golgotha ("The Skull") where He was to be crucified. Notice that Jesus does not say any words of disapproval to the evildoers surrounding Him like a pack of wolves.

Lastly, we meditate on the **Crucifixion of Jesus**. Once again, He does not reproach the soldiers who hammer nails into His hands and feet.

And so through meditating on the Sorrowful Mysteries we learn the virtue of Humility. Not just earthly humility, but Humility with a capital "H" kind of Humility; divine Humility.

FIRST SORROWFUL MYSTERY
THE AGONY OF OUR LORD
IN THE GARDEN

"Father, if You are willing, remove this chalice from Me; nevertheless, not My will, but Yours be done."
~Luke 22:42

My Precious Jesus, what great Humility You have! If it be Thy will, please grant this perfect Humility to me. Give me the grace to do anything You ask of me. I want to be one with You for all eternity.

Have you ever suffered? Of course you have; all humans do at some point. Even Jesus suffered! He suffered persecutions and being mocked; He suffered heavy blows that tore His skin apart. He suffered nails being hammered into His hands and feet. He suffered for you and for me.

Just imagine what He must have felt: First of all, here in the Garden of Gethsemane, He took on all of the sins—past, present, <u>and</u> future—of the entire world upon His sorrowful soul. It weighed Him down, as He was human like us. (Remember, Jesus had two natures: human and divine, meaning that although He was really 100% man he was also 100% God at the same time.) You know that feeling before you go into the confessional? Your shoulders seem to droop down; your head feels heavy. Every movement you make seems painful because you know you have hurt Our Lord and you are ashamed. Well, multiply that feeling about a million times and you have what Jesus felt. Our poor, beautiful Jesus Who only ever loved EVERYONE!

The prophet Isaiah said (long before Jesus' birth), *"Ours were the sufferings He bore, ours the sorrows He carried." (Isaiah 53:4)*

There is a church song I love called *"Beautiful Savior."* One of the lines goes, *"How beautiful, the heart that bled; that took all my sin, and bore it instead."* How true and touching! Jesus took all of your sins and bore them for you to save you from the fiery grips of the devil. Of course that doesn't mean you don't have to go to confession; you still do and should try to go often. To be a faithful Catholic you must confess at least once a year, particularly during the Easter time; but some Priests recommend monthly—and even weekly—confession. Why? Because we are all sinners and we are all thirsting for the sanctifying grace we obtain when we make a good confession. Even the pope goes to confession EVERY DAY!

Every intentional bad thought or desire or thing we do should be confessed, because we should be truly sorry for anything we could have done that would cause Jesus any sorrow. They say that when we sin, we nail Jesus to the cross all over again.

In His apparitions to St. Margaret Mary Alacoque, Jesus once told her "I would create the whole universe again, just to hear you say that you love Me."

If we truly love Jesus, let's make a pact that we'll try to always do as He would want, and when we experience pain, suffering, and disappointment (which happens A LOT) we'll offer it up for the poor souls in purgatory who have no one to pray for them, and remember what Jesus went through in the garden of Gethsemane.

SECOND SORROWFUL MYSTERY
THE SCOURGING AT THE PILLAR

"'Truth?' said Pilate, 'What is that?' and with that he went out again to the Jews and said, 'I find no case against Him. So I shall have Him flogged and then let Him go.' Pilate then had Jesus taken and scourged."
~John 18:38; Luke 23:15,16; John 19:1

My Precious Jesus, *"Despised and rejected by men, a Man of sorrows, harshly dealt with, [You] bore it humbly, like a lamb that is led to the slaughterhouse." (Isaiah 53:3; 53:7)* Help me to bear wrongs as patiently as You did, and to find good in everyone I meet, even when they are rude to me.

Once again Jesus shows us His perfect Humility. Pilate was blind to good, beautiful things. The Truth he asks about is standing in front of him and he doesn't even realize it! Oftentimes we are like Pilate; blind to the Truth. Sometimes we blind ourselves to escape the judgments of God, forgetting that He is all-knowing and all-merciful. When we steer towards the wrong road we should pause and remember when Jesus was scourged for us. Think of the pain—they slashed Him over and over with a whip!

Many times it happens that we see our peers dress in immodest clothing and we figure we should do the same. Let's look at our sorrowful, bleeding Jesus as an inspiration to do the opposite—to pray for them and cover what should be covered for His sake. How proud He'll be of us!

"On Him lies a punishment that brings us peace, and through His wounds we are healed." (Isaiah 53:5).

Remember that Isaiah the prophet lived and died before Jesus' time. Through the Holy Spirit he prophesied all about the Crucifixion. God is amazing!

THIRD SORROWFUL MYSTERY

THE CROWNING WITH THORNS

"And having twisted some thorns into a crown, they put this on His Head and placed a reed in His right hand. To make fun of Him they knelt down to Him, saying, 'Hail, King of the Jews!' and they spat on Him, and took the reed and struck Him on the Head."
~Matthew 27:29-30

My Precious Jesus, help me to never treat anyone the way the Roman soldiers treated You. Let me not hurt with actions or words that I say or that I don't say. Help me to never judge or despise anyone, and especially help me to never treat You in this manner.

There's a funny little word that's been quite prominent in the teen world today.

It's a myth called perfection.
Guess what?
It doesn't exist on earth.
In fact, it's so nonexistent it's almost hilarious.

ALL of us human beings have faults, but God does not; and that is why only Heaven can be perfect.

It hurts to not "fit in." Maybe you seem different from the rest of your friends because of the way you talk or dress. Maybe you like movies or books or music that is completely different from what everyone else likes. But everybody's SUPPOSED to be different! Every human being is completely unique; no fingerprint can ever be repeated (unless God willed it so, of course.) A lot of people don't get that, and sometimes people (even good ones) can be mean and say things that are less than nice. All these things are a kind of suffering and we should offer them to God united to Jesus' suffering on the cross. If Jesus Christ, the Lord of all the earth, was ridiculed, spat upon and crowned with sharp thorns, then how much more worthy are *we* to be teased and made fun of!

Try not to focus on the bad things people say or do, and always remember and meditate on this third Sorrowful Mystery.

FOURTH SORROWFUL MYSTERY
THE CARRYING OF THE CROSS

"So they took Jesus, and He went out, bearing His own cross." ~John 19:17

My Precious Jesus, You said *"If anyone wants to be a follower of Mine, let him renounce himself and take up his cross every day and follow Me." (Luke 9:23)* Help me to take up my cross, whatever it may be, and follow You every day of my life. If it be Your will, give me the graces I need to bear any sufferings that may come my way.

Jesus told us to take up our cross every day; not just once in a while. The road to Heaven is full of many sufferings, but if we bear them for the years this earthly life lasts, we will have nothing but happiness and peace for all eternity. Sounds like a pretty good deal, right?

We don't have to go out of our way to find sufferings to undergo for the love of Jesus.

Sufferings come in all different sizes. A small one might be denying yourself that extra piece of pizza or not having sweets. Larger ones could be dealing patiently with health problems, being made fun of, or loneliness. Whatever your suffering(s) may be, bear them humbly and don't be like the hypocrisy-laden Pharisees in the Bible who neglect their appearance so as to look as if they are fasting, or pray only in the temples so everyone can see them and think they're such great people.

"When you pray, go into your room and pray in secret." (Matthew 6:6)

FIFTH SORROWFUL MYSTERY
THE CRUCIFIXION AND DEATH OF
OUR LORD

"When they reached the place called The Skull they crucified Him. Near the cross of Jesus stood His Mother and the disciple He loved. Jesus said to His Mother, 'Woman, behold your son.' Then to the disciple He said, 'Behold, your Mother.' And Jesus cried out in a loud voice, 'Father, into Your hands I commit My spirit.' And bowing His head, He breathed His last."
~Luke 23:33; John 19:25-27; Luke 23:46; John19:30

My Precious Jesus, please give me Your heart, so that I may never fill it with impure things but You and You Alone. Give me Your eyes, so that I may never judge others' appearances. Give me Your feet, that I may walk humbly, carrying my cross every day with Your blessed smile upon my face. Give me Your hands, so that I may always help those in need with the

kind of love only You can give. Help me
to obtain Eternal life because I know
that without You, I am mere dust.

So first of all, Jesus is the King of the Universe and WE put Him to death with our sins. Secondly, after three days in the tomb He rose from the dead. For many people today this is hard to believe. We are told that it is impossible, but *"With God ALL things ARE possible."* *(Matthew 19:26)* Although it seems in the Gospel that the Roman soldiers crucified Jesus, He was really crucified by our sins. Just as He took all the sins of the world upon Himself in the Garden of Gethsemane, He continues to carry them as He walks up to the place called The Skull. There He is to be stripped of His clothing, beaten, and nailed, hands and feet, to the cross, and hung to die for three long hours.

Even when in great pain and torment, Our Lord's words are charitable and forgiving, and not once does He even make the slightest complaint.

Here at the foot of the cross He gave us Mary as our Mother—He didn't just give her to the disciple John, but every single one of us. We need to take this special gift of God that is Mary and honor her every day.

Years ago, one of my best friends, Fr. Philip Acquaro, told a story at Mass. He said that a man died, weighed down by heavy crosses, and came to Jesus and said "Lord, why did You give me so many crosses in my life? See, other people only got one or two, but I got so many." Jesus then pointed to his tiniest cross, so small it could barely be seen. "This is the one *I* gave you." He said.

How many times do we bring crosses upon <u>ourselves!</u> Ralph Waldo Emerson once said, "Most of the shadows of this life are caused by standing in one's own sunshine."

Jesus only gives us as much as we can handle. He would never give us more than we could deal with; we sometimes do that to ourselves. He loves us all very deeply.

The Glorious Mysteries

(to be recited on Sundays and Wednesdays)

In the Glorious Mysteries we meditate on the **Resurrection** of Jesus, which is the greatest event in all of history.

We also reflect on the **Ascension**, when Jesus rose into Heaven forty days after the resurrection.

We meditate on the **Descent of the Holy Spirit,** in which the Holy Spirit came to the apostles. This was the birth of the Catholic Church.

We contemplate the **Assumption** of our Blessed Mother, when she was assumed into Heaven.

Lastly, we reflect on the **Coronation,** when Mary was crowned the Queen of Heaven and earth.

FIRST GLORIOUS MYSTERY
THE RESURRECTION OF OUR LORD

*"He has risen from the dead; come and
see the place where He lay."
~Matthew 28:6-7*

My Glorified Lord, help me
to believe all the truths of the Holy
Catholic Church, no matter how complex
or difficult they may seem. You taught
them to me; You Who knows everything;
help me to explain these truths to others.

How often in life do we say
"That's not fair!" The same can be said
about the Crucifixion. Jesus, completely
innocent died such a gruesome death,
and all He ever did was love <u>everyone!</u>
But He is God, and He can do everything.
And so He saved us from our sins
through his death and Resurrection,
and now gives us a glimpse into our
own resurrection. In the Nicene Creed
at Mass we say *"We believe in the
resurrection of the dead."* We will all be
raised from the dead someday. The
people who lived virtuous and holy lives
will have beautiful bodies and live

happily with God forever, but the people who lived evil, impure, and worldly lives and never gave God a second thought will have suffering for eternity. It's our choice.

Even the disciples, who were afraid that they too would be crucified if anyone found out that they were followers of Jesus, were hiding in a room for the three days while Jesus was in the tomb. Some didn't even believe it when Mary Magdalene told them Jesus had risen from the dead! They were men like us with intellect and free will, and they chose to believe what they wanted to—that is, until Jesus appeared to them in Person!

SECOND GLORIOUS MYSTERY
THE ASCENSION OF OUR
LORD INTO HEAVEN

"And so the Lord Jesus was taken up into Heaven, there at the right hand of God He took His place."
~Mark 16:19

♥ My Glorious Lord, I know that it must have been hard for Your Mother Mary and the disciples to see You ascend into Heaven to take Your place at the right hand of God. They must have been worried about what would become of them if You were to leave the earth. But You are a loving God and refuse to leave us as orphans. Help me to find You everywhere, because You *are* everywhere.

Mark 16:19 tells us that Jesus was taken up into Heaven, and took His place at the right hand of God. Luke 24:51 says, *"As He blessed them, He parted from them and was taken up into Heaven."* So the all-knowing God didn't just die, resurrect Himself, and ascend into Heaven without showing us once again the virtue of Charity. (Yes, with a capital "C.") He gave us His blessing. This great gift and blessing of God, which we will meditate on in the next mystery, is the Holy Spirit.

Let's pray that, through these next ten Hail Marys, the Holy Spirit may move and breathe in all of God's children, that they may always do good and never any evil, especially for those who misuse the glorious gift that is their body.

THIRD GLORIOUS MYSTERY
THE DESCENT OF THE HOLY SPIRIT

"When the day of Pentecost had come, they were all together in one place. Suddenly a sound came from Heaven, like a mighty wind. They were all filled with the Holy Spirit, and began to speak about the mighty works of God."
~Acts 2:1-2; 4; 11

Prayer to the Holy Spirit by St. Augustine: Breathe into me, Holy Spirit, that my thoughts may all be holy. Move in me, Holy Spirit, that my work too may be holy. Attract my heart, Holy Spirit, that I may love only what is holy. Strengthen me, Holy Spirit, that I may defend all that is holy. Protect me, Holy Spirit, that I always may be holy. Amen.

It must have been hard to be one of the original twelve (or eleven *faithful*) disciples of Jesus. They had to deal with persecutions and ridicule from their fellow people on a regular basis, (and all but St. John were martyred for their faith in Jesus Christ). It's no surprise that for nine days after Jesus ascended into Heaven they were hiding in a room wondering what to do. They're a lot like us in a way. Although we may be good and faithful Catholics who love God above all else, we may be afraid of what others might do to us, making us shy away from telling others about Jesus. This is what happened to the disciples. They sat, afraid of the imminent persecutions, trials and tribulations; afraid of being without Jesus. But Jesus didn't desert them. He sent them the Holy Spirit, Who still breathes through the Catholic Church today.

How awesome and charitable our God is, He Who would never leave us as orphans but gives us instead His great gift of love and mercy.

FOURTH GLORIOUS MYSTERY
THE ASSUMPTION OF
THE BLESSED VIRGIN

"Now a great sign appeared in Heaven: A woman, adorned with the sun. She was standing on the moon, with the twelve stars on her head for a crown. With jewels set in gold, and dressed in brocades, the King's daughter is led in to the King."
~Revelations 12:1; Psalm 45:13,14

♥ My Blessed Lady, how beautiful your Assumption must have been! I can see it as if I had been there: Going up to Heaven body and soul and then you stood next to your Son, with twelve stars (representing the twelve disciples) as a crown on your lovely head. Your garments were resplendent with the day's sun and covered with jewels set in gold and brocades. My mother, *"show me your face, let me hear your voice; for your voice is sweet and your face is beautiful."*
(Song 2:14)

"The trust you have shown shall not pass from the memories of men, but shall ever remind them of the power of God." (Judith 13:25)

What a wonderful model for us to follow! Instead of watching what celebrities do, we should pay special attention to everything the Blessed Mother did. The trust of the Blessed Virgin Mary surpasses the trust of any person that ever lived, is living, or ever will live for all of time. Some people think Mary's "Yes" to God in the Magnificat (also commonly called the *Fiat*) was her only "Yes." That's not true; Mary had to say "Yes" to God's will when searching for Jesus in the temple. She had to say "Yes" to God when Jesus worked His first miracle at the Wedding in Cana. Mary certainly had to say a big "Yes" to God when she saw her Son hanging lifeless on the Cross. She had to say "Yes" when she held the crucified Body of her Son in her arms, just as she had when He was a tender Infant. She had to say "Yes" when Jesus ascended into Heaven. She truly lived her own words: *"Let it be done to me according to Thy will." (Luke 1:38)*

Mary never lived her own will; she only knew how to live God's. Jesus showed so much respect for His mother. We should imitate Him. And we should imitate His mother. What a woman she was! The most perfect, beautiful, peaceful, loving person ever born; the greatest role model any of us could ever have to follow!

"Come then, my love; my lovely one, come." (Song of Solomon 2:10)

FIFTH GLORIOUS MYSTERY
THE CORONATION OF
THE BLESSED VIRGIN

"Who is this arising like the dawn, fair as the moon, resplendent as the sun? Like the rainbow gleaming against brilliant clouds, like blossoms in the days of spring."
~Song 6:10; Ecclus 50:7-8

My Blessed Lady, My Mother, how beautiful you are! Many people ridicule and disrespect women today through television, movies, music, magazines, the internet, and the way in which they speak of them. But your Son shows us through your Coronation how women are to be treated; as the gifts of God that they are. O Woman of all women! I love you with all my heart. Help me to be like you and help all people—men and women alike—to have great respect for the glorious bodies God gave them.

Mary's trust isn't the only amazing thing about her. Another virtue she mastered was Charity. Every day of her earthly life she gave of herself, as God's handmaid, so that whatever He needed to be done would be done through her.

"Approach me, you who desire me, and take your fill of my fruits." (Ecclus 24:19)

Mary never did anything for herself; everything she ever did was for her Family in Nazareth. And she continues to pour herself out for us today.

Remember—Catholic's don't worship Mary. Worship is reserved for God alone. We venerate and honor her because she bore Jesus Christ in her womb and because Jesus, God the Father and the Holy Spirit honor her. She is our mother and our intercessor. Certainly Jesus loves to grant favors to us through His Blessed Mother! She certainly is the most perfect woman who ever lived!

"And now, my children, listen to me; listen to instruction and learn to be wise. For those who find me find life,

and win favor from the Lord."
(Proverbs 8:32; 33; 35)

ACKNOWLEDGEMENTS:

Where do I begin?! So many wonderful people helped me in getting this book in your hands!

First and foremost, thank you to Mrs. Sherry Boas, a wonderful author and a very holy woman that is a great mother to her children, a great friend of mine, and a great inspiration to all Catholics with her superb writing. It sounds cliché, but I absolutely could not have done this without her. It was through her patient prodding that I finally achieved my dream of becoming an author, and I will never forget her for that.

Thank you, of course, to my Mom and Dad. Thank you for believing in me and praying for me and raising me the way you did. I know I haven't exactly been the easiest child in the world to parent, but I hope you know that your tireless efforts have been well worth it, for had it not been for your help and encouragement and the education you have blessed me with, this book would never been made a reality.

Thank you to my sister Jackie for being a stalwart editor and the punctuation queen! Thank you to my brother-in-law, Nick for knowing how to turn anything into a JPEG! That saved me so much stress. Thank you to my darling "Chubba Dubba," Austin. You're the best nephew I could've ever dreamed of having and you bring out so many words and so much joy from within me with your adorable smile. My heart literally melts every time you call me "Asche." Thank you to my sister Jill and her soon-to-be husband, Jake, for all of the laughs and fun memories you've brought into my life and also for all of your prayers. Thank you to my Grandma and Nanny, because you have both cheered this project on so thoroughly and it makes me so proud to call you my grandmothers. Grandpa DeMato and Grandpa Belle-Oudry, I felt your prayers for me every time I sat down to write. I cannot wait to meet you two in Heaven someday.

Thank you to the rest of my huge family, all my aunts and uncles and cousins! And to Kathy Richard, Sylvia Acuña, Mary Sarrantonio, and Kathy Stover, four incredible women that have brought much happiness to my life. Thank you to all of you daily communicants who I love to see each morning. You all inspire me with your profound love of God and I enjoy your company more than you'll ever know.

Thank you to all of the wonderful priests who have inspired me throughout my years; Fr. Philip Acquaro, Fr. Steven Kunkel, Fr. Kilian McCaffrey, Fr. Charlie Goraieb, Fr. Thomas Bennett, and Fr. Jess Ty. You all mean so much to me and have brought me closer to God.

Thank You, Jesus, for giving Your Blessed Mother Mary to me on the Cross when You said "Behold, your mother!" (Jn 19:27). And thank You, God, for putting all of those wonderful people I mentioned above into my life! You have blessed me with so many good friends throughout the years, many of whom I haven't mentioned because if I did it would take up an entire chapter. To all of those, thank you for being my friends!

Lastly, here's to you, the reader of this book. Thank you for believing in me. You'll never know how much it means to me that you read my very first book.

~Grace

Grace E. Belle-Oudry is a Catholic teenager who has an avid interest in World War II and reviewing classic cinema. When she's not reading books and watching movies, she's *writing* books and *writing* movies. With aspirations of becoming a screenwriter and film director, her favorite movie is *On the Waterfront*. Grace enjoys ballet, playing tennis, going to daily Mass, making people laugh with her merciless wit, and watching 70's sitcoms. Her favorite author is Margaret Mitchell.